GW00535914

From Africa:

A celebration of creativity from Africa, compiled and published by Counter-Print

First published in 2022 © Counter-Print
ISBN 978-1-915392-00-8 Designed by Counter-Print
Printed in China

With special thanks to all the contributors.

5 Hust Wilson

13 Thandiwe Muriu

21 Elio Moavero

29 Thabiso Ntuli

41 Vukile Batyi

47 Pearly Yon

55 Mam'Gobozi Design Factory

63 Daniel Ting Chong

75 The Ninevites

81 Mrs + Mr Luke

95 Blood, Sweat + Polony

103 R!OT — Sindiso Nyoni

111 Bold Branding

119 Studio Onss Mhirsi

131 Ahmad Hammoud

139 VM DSGN

151 David Alabo

159 MUTI

The vast, beautiful continent of Africa contains 54 countries, covers 6% of the Earth's total surface area and, with 1.3 billion people, accounts for about 16% of the world's population. Africa has the youngest population of all the continents and, despite a low concentration of wealth, recent economic expansion is making it an important economic market — its cities are amongst the fastest-growing in the world.

The vastness of Africa's geography and its cultural diversity (not to mention the many national, regional, religious and linguistic boundaries) contradict the notion of Africa as one entity. Its many, diverse countries are sources of vibrant design and African influences are seen in art and culture around the world. However, there is no one 'African style' and we should refrain from generalising a continent of such vast scale. The continent's design output is not limited to a single aesthetic or singular history; rather it is multifaceted and influenced by the context in which the designer lives — locally and globally.

Myths of a singular language connected to African design have begun to be replaced over recent years, with archaic stereotypes of poverty and inequity shifting to stories of innovation, resourcefulness and optimism. Visually, it's design had also too often fallen victim to stereotype, represented by ethnic prints, earthy colours and textures. In 2009, Chimamanda Ngozi Adichie spoke on 'The Danger of a Single Story' which has become one of the top ten most-viewed TED Talks of all time.

However, Africa's young, self-confident creative scene is helping to rewrite its own story. Moving on from externally imposed definitions, they seem to draw inspiration from their rich and varied cultures, while remaining open to global influences and technology, combining both tradition and modernity to create something entirely new.

Although European, American and Asian influences are absorbed, in comparison to Western design, which is greatly influenced by minimalism, African design has its own sense of style, humour and cultural history which make it unique. While colour, pattern and craft are profoundly rooted in African heritage, contemporary African design is also innovative as well as traditional. A new generation of designers are creating change by kickstarting businesses and projects in innovative professional sectors with the SiliconCape being an economic example of the manifestation of this shift.

This combination of tradition and modernity is evident within the work included in this book. Old techniques are given a contemporary aesthetic by the likes of the Ninevites, who call on a wealth of textile history in Africa to create their cutting-edge designs for pillows, throws and artworks. Other designers tell the story of their surroundings by creating unique art such as Vukile Mavumengwana (VM DSGN) whose 'South African Greeting Cards' use iconic designs of popular household products to communicate all kinds of different messages. These designs are executed in a collage-like manner, a style that is well-established in townships in South Africa, especially to decorate the interiors of humble abodes. Meanwhile, the photographer Thandiwe Muriu has made a name for herself well beyond Africa's borders — creating strikingly modern fashion photography containing African fabric designs.

Messages of hope, tolerance and inclusivity are common themes within the book. Thabiso Ntuli's publication design for the National Condom Communication Strategy, VM DSGN's 'ZA Rights' merchandise collection advocating for social justice or MUTI's typographic campaign for The Hope Factory all suggest a design community with a social conscience and togetherness.

Design in Africa seems to be thriving and this new wave of African creatives are making a name for themselves globally. Helping with this are a number of key initiatives that African designers are undeniably benefiting from: the Pan Afrikan Design Institute (PADI) and other organisations such as Afrikan Design Matters, Design Indaba, Dakar Biennale and the Black Artists & Designers Guild (BADG) for example, are all respected institutions on the global creative landscape who have helped to encourage the promotion of creativity from this continent.

This book is our attempt to explore and celebrate Africa's creative energy, inspiration and artistic community as part of our ongoing series on regions and their creative output. We hope you will find inspiration within its pages.

Jon Dowling
Counter-Print

Hust Wilson

Live More Worry Less. Self-initiated lettering. 2021.

From Africa

hustwilson.com

Heart
—
Self-initiated illustration
2021

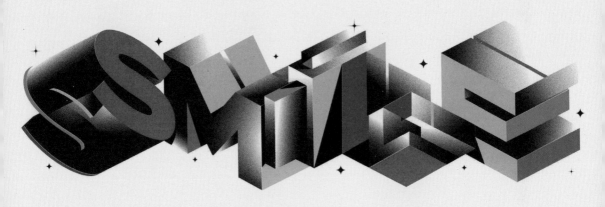

Smile
—
Self-initiated lettering
2021

Facebook (Meta)
'Education' lettering designed for
a technology conglomerate
2021

Men's Health

'How to Change a Life' lettering
designed for a magazine
2018

Adobe Inc.

'Trust' lettering designed for
a computer software company
2021

It's Okay. Okay.
Self-initiated lettering
2021

You Can

Self-initiated lettering
2021

Thandiwe Muriu

From Africa

thandiwemuriu.com

Camo 11

© Thandiwe Muriu
2021

Camo 13

© Thandiwe Muriu
2021

Camo 20

© Thandiwe Muriu

2021

Camo 23

© Thandiwe Muriu

2021

Camo 27   Child's Play 2

© Thandiwe Muriu   © Thandiwe Muriu

2021   2018

Child's Play 3
Created as part of a live feature on CNN
© Thandiwe Muriu
2018

Elio Moavero

Loeries. Poster design for an annual advertising awards. 2021.

From Africa

eliomoavero.com

CRAFT BRONZE

DESIGN

LIVE COMMUNICATION

CRAFT CERTIFICATE

DIGITAL Crafts

DESIGN Crafts

DIGITAL COMMUNICATION

INTEGRATED CAMPAIGN

FILM

FILM Crafts

EFFECTIVE CREATIVITY

Marketing LEADERSHIP And INNOVATION

MEDIA INNOVATION

PR And MEDIA COMMUNICATION

YOUNG CREATIVES

RADIO And AUDIO

RADIO Crafts

USA NON-ENGLISH RADIO

Service DESIGN

AGENCY Of The YEAR

Loeries
Lettering for an annual advertising awards
2021

THE REVIVAL CO PRESENTS:

BUY THE TICKET

TAKE THE RIDE

13 NOVEMBER 2021
DISTRICT 61A HARRINGTON STREET

DJ INVIZABLE · THE LOOSE ENDS · HARTLEYVALE

THE KARRIERS · LOS SUEÑOS · DJ PHIL KRAMER (AFTER HOURS)

GLITCH CULTURE · HONEST BURGERS · ROASTIN' RECORDS · ART EXHIBITION
FILM SCREENINGS · BEER PONG w/FOKOF LAGER

Elio Moavero

←

Buy The Ticket Take The Ride
_____
Poster design for The Revival Co,
a host of live music events
2021

Jimmy O. Yang
_____
Poster design for an actor,
comedian & writer
2019

Metallica
_____
Poster design for a metal band
2021

The Late Night Arcade

Poster design for a weekly gaming night

2019

Thabiso Ntuli

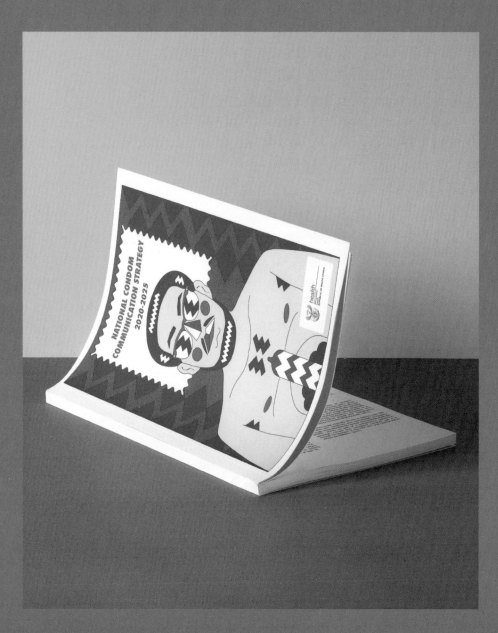

National Condom Communication Strategy. Publication design for the United Nations Population Fund (UNFPA). 2020.

From Africa

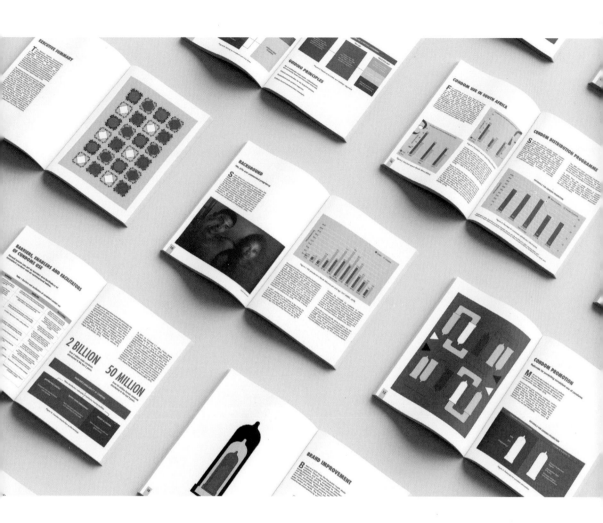

National Condom

Communication Strategy

Publication design for the United
Nations Population Fund (UNFPA)
2020

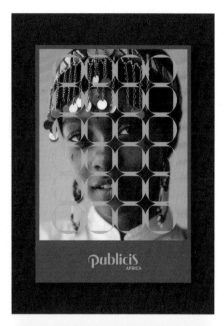

Publicis Africa

Branding for an advertising agency

2021

Thabiso Ntuli

Russian Bear
Merchandise design
for an alcohol brand
2020

Thabiso Ntuli

Meet Visa AFCON

Campaign for a financial
service provider
2021

Talk Amongst Yourselves
Branding for a podcast
2021

Vukile Batyi

Botho Project Space. Editorial design for an art gallery. 2020.

From Africa

vukile-batyi.studio

Botho Project Space

Editorial & tote bag design
for an art gallery
2020

Vukile Batyi

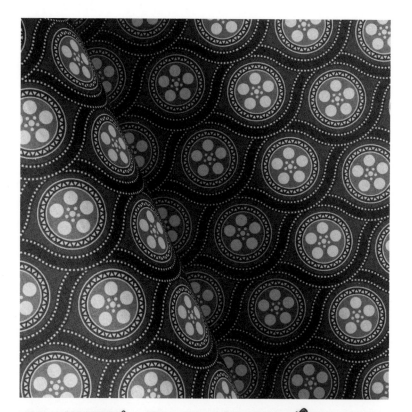

KZN Film
Textile design for a film festival
2014

"The Passion of Muhammad" II
Self-initiated textile design
2020

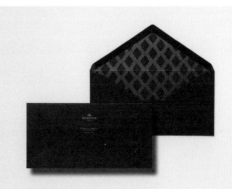

Abantwana Belanga – Children of the Son

Cover design for a band

Pearly Yon

Capetown Postcards. Illustration for gift wrap. 2017.

From Africa

pearlyyon.com

CAMPS BAY

CAPE TOWN

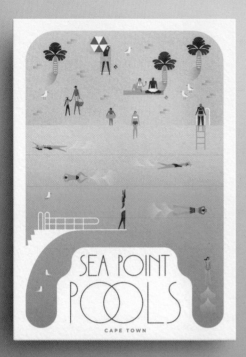

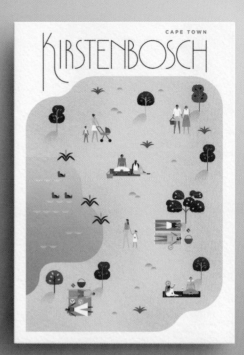

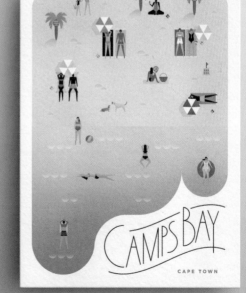

Capetown Postcards

Self-initiated postcards
2017

Pearly Yon

Bonnie & Clyde – First Batch
Packaging design for a distillery
2014

↘

Bonnie & Clyde – Second Batch
Packaging design for a distillery
2016

Delphis Wine Labels

Wine labels designed for Hamilton Russel
Vineyards on behalf of Nimb Hotel
2013

Never by Doubt

Poster design for Jason Knight
2017

Mam'Gobozi
Design Factory

Roots Rock Reggae. Identity for an annual music festival. 2016.

Roots Rock Reggae. Identity for an annual music festival. 2016.

From Africa

ARTISTS
Gran'Mah (Mozambique)
Kingfisha (Australia)
Urban Village (South Africa)
Malcolm Jiyane ft Stop Nocents
& Sifiso (The Mûrfînz)

ROOTS
ROCK
REGGAE

25
MAY
2016

mamgobozidesign.com

Roots Rock Reggae

Identity for an annual music festival

2016

Easy Sundays Productions

Branding for a film production company
2017

The Africa Centre
Branding for a non-profit
organisation
2021

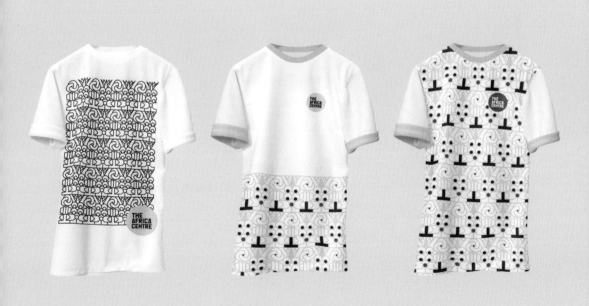

KIZA Agency

Branding for a creative
management company
2021

Daniel Ting Chong

Jin Gin. Branding & packaging design for a liquor brand. 2019.

From Africa

danieltingchong.com

Jin Gin

Branding & packaging design
for a liquor brand
2019

65

Daniel Ting Chong

ASICS Rugby World Cup
Campaign for a sportswear brand
2019

LOCAL
———
Branding for a brewery
2019

Dear Maria Café

Branding for a coffee shop
2018

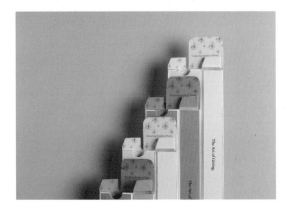

1701
—
Branding for a luxury nougat
2020

Design Indaba
Identity for a design festival
2019

OkayAfrica
Pattern design for an African-
focused media agency
2017

The Ninevites

Mangaliso Rug. Handwoven rug with sheep wool. 2020.

From Africa

Karoo Rug & Thandiswa Artwork

Handwoven rug with sheep
wool and an artwork designed
in collaboration with Jo Elbourne
2020

Kinshasa Cushion

Handwoven cushion with
sheep wool
2020

Congo Cushions

Handwoven cushion with
sheep wool
2020

Sankara Rug
Handwoven rug with sheep wool
2020

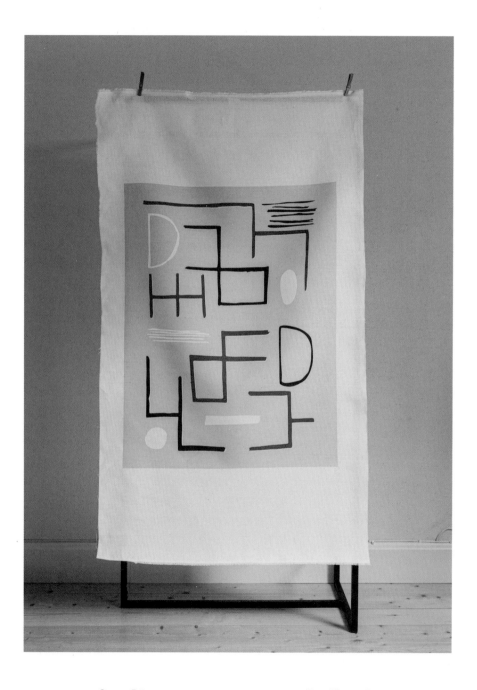

Congo Print

Silk screened on 100% organic hemp
2020

Pan African Print

Silk screened on 100% organic hemp
2020

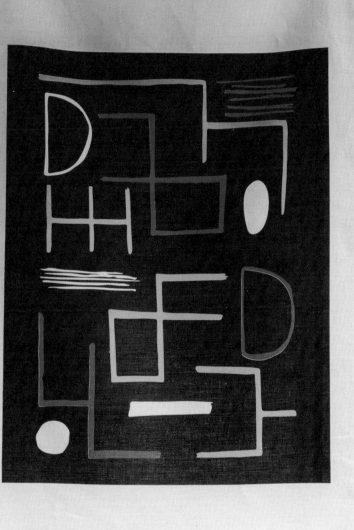

Imitha Rug
Handwoven rug with 100% mohair

Mrs + Mr Luke

Southern Guild. Artwork for a gallery. 2016.

From Africa

mrsandmrluke.com

deCOLOURnise – Black and White

Artworks for Michaelis School
of Fine Art
2018

Gesiggies 6
Artwork for Jenn Singer Gallery
2019

Gesiggies 7

Artwork for Jenn Singer Gallery
2019

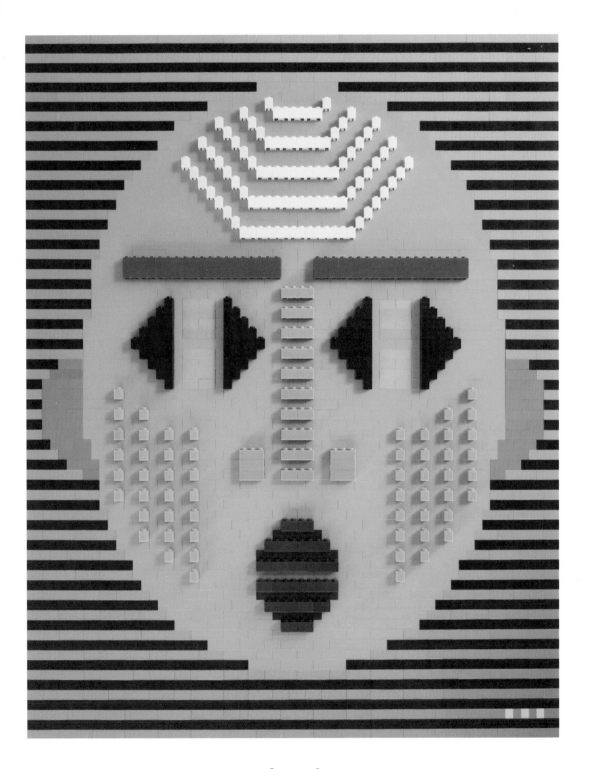

Gesiggies 8
Artwork for Jenn Singer Gallery
2019

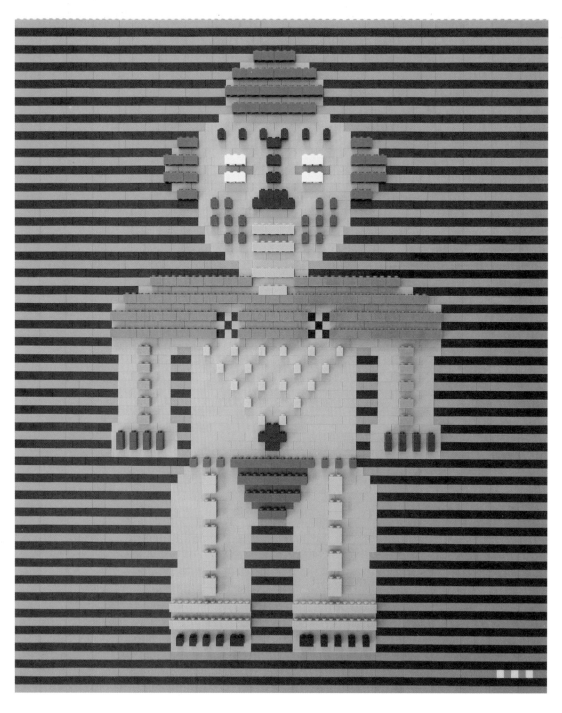

Jelly Baby He
Artwork for WorldArt Gallery
2020

Jelly Baby She
Artwork for WorldArt Gallery
2020

Elements&Compounds – Noise,
Transform & Unite
Artworks for Eclectica
Contemporary Gallery
2018

→
Elements&Compounds – Collide
Artwork for Eclectica
Contemporary Gallery
2018

Halls Bus Shelters
'Own the Moment' campaign
for sweet company Halls
2018

Reflections of a Queen – Ashanti Grey,
Ashanti Pink, Wolof Blue & Yoruba Grey
Artworks for WorldArt Gallery
2018

Blood, Sweat + Polony

Assembly. Branding for a collective space. 2018.

From Africa

YOU'RE INVITED.

Assembly
Branding for a collective space
2018

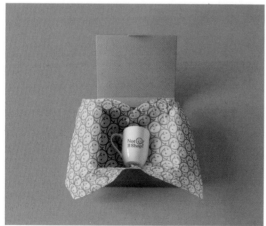

Not-a-Shop!

Branding for a concept store
2018

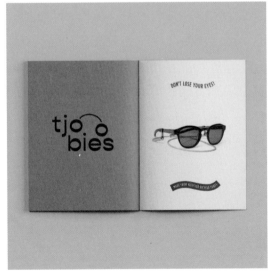

Tjoobies
Branding for a leather goods manufacturer
2020

R!OT – Sindiso Nyoni

Converse: ZA #CreateAtHome. Design for a sneaker & apparel brand. 2020.

From Africa

studioriot.com

Get Out
Poster design for Jordan Peele,
Universal Pictures/Monkeypaw
Productions
2017

Scribbled in Red
Poster design for independent
filmmaker Khule Mayisa,
2020

OKUMHLOPHE
Poster design for independent
filmmaker Khule Mayisa
2021

The Banishment
Poster design for independent
filmmaker Twiggy Matiwana
2021

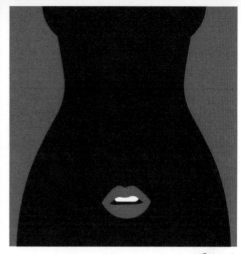

Scribbled in Red
A Film by Khule Mayisa

DIRECTED BY KHULE MAYISA PRODUCED BY KHULE MAYISA
SHOT BY KHULE MAYISA EDITED BY KHULE MAYISA
POEM BY DOMINIQUE CHRISTINA
STARRING NOLWAZI MADALANE

Starring Paballo Mokwena, Bontle Bing and Khule Mayisa
OKUMHLOPHE
Written, Directed & Produced by Khule Mayisa Music by Katlego Tladi

THE BANISH MENT
A POWERFUL SHEDOW

Caltex
Mural design for a petroleum
brand/gas station franchise
2018

Stella Artois x Sindiso N. –
Pure Malt Pure Art
Installations for a beer brand
2021

Converse: ZA #CreateAtHome

Design for a sneaker & apparel brand
2020

Bold Branding

From Africa

bold-branding.com

Bold Branding

Voilà Dessert Shop

Packaging for an ice cream range
2021

Notch Artisanal Bistro
Branding for a restaurant
2018

Bold Branding

NOTCH
Branding for an artisanal bistro
2019

Studio Onss Mhirsi

Pirata Group. Branding for a restaurant. 2019.

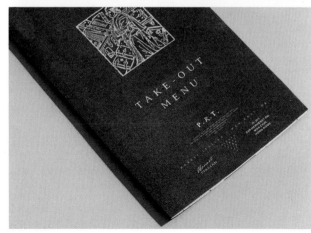

Pirata
Branding for a restaurant
2019

Chamboule Tout

Art direction proposal for
The Trophée Presse Citron BNF
2017

Credits
Marine Dion, Anaelle Barnier,
Marie Anne Barjoux

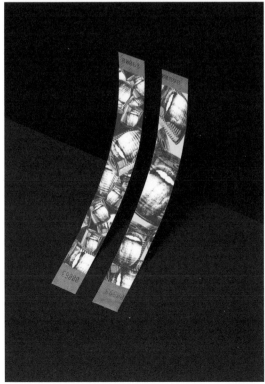

Rêvons.

30-08
30-08
Oct-No

نحلم فنحيا

Vivons!

MINISTÈRE DES AFFAIRES CULTURELLES

CNCI

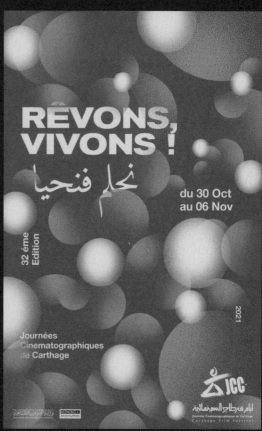

Ahmad Hammoud

From Africa

hammoud3000.com

Cinema El Housh

Identity for an independent
art-house cinema. Designed in
collaboration with Nora Aly.
2020

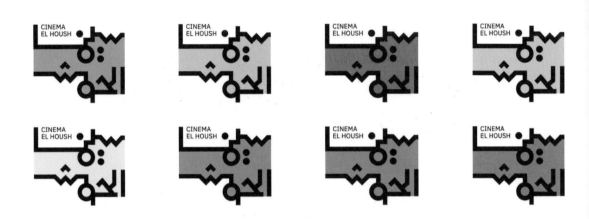

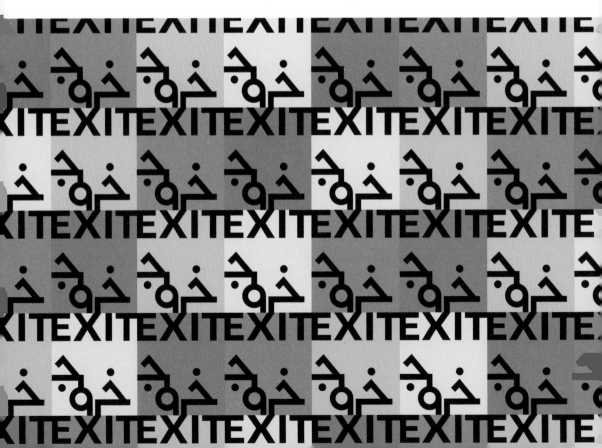

CINEMA EL HOUSH

العودة إلى سينما الحوش

BACK TO COURTYARD CINEMAS

24
06
19

Ministry of Culture
وزارة الثقافة

عليان شعبين، أقدم بروجيكشونست محلي - جدة ١٩٧٨

يونيو
يوليو
٢٠١٩

جدول الأفلام

01- 2001 A SPACE ODYSSEY by Stanley Kubrick

02- SHOPLIFTERS by Hirokazu Kore-eda

03- YOMEDDINE by Abou Bakr Shawky

04- THE BICYCLE THIEF by Vittorio De Sica

05- COLD WAR by Paweł Pawlikowski

06- إسكندرية...ليه؟ by Youssef Chahine

07- 8 ½ by Federico Fellini

08- DILILI À PARIS by Michel Ocelot

09- عروس الشعر by Abdulrahman Khawj

10- عمرة و العرس الثاني by Mahmoud Sabbagh

جميع العروض تبدأ الساعة ٩:١٥ مساءً

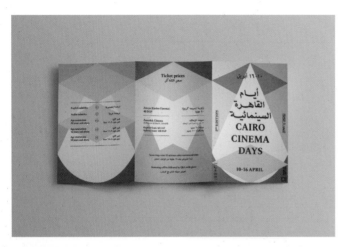

Identity for Zawya Cinema. Designed
in collaboration with Nora Aly.
2019

Cairo Cinema Days

Identity for Zawya Cinema. Designed
in collaboration with Nora Aly.
2019

→
FRACTAL
Poster design for a party promoter
2019

FRACTAL

CCC 18th FLOOR

GONNO
& FKHMY
NOUS
+MHMHMH.INFO

THU 13 FEB

9 PM - LATE

VM DSGN

From Africa

WINNER OF 9 INTERNATIONAL & 6 NATIONAL AWARDS

behance.net/vums

TotalEnergies AFCON Jersey

Design for the 'TotalEnergies
Football Together' jersey
2021

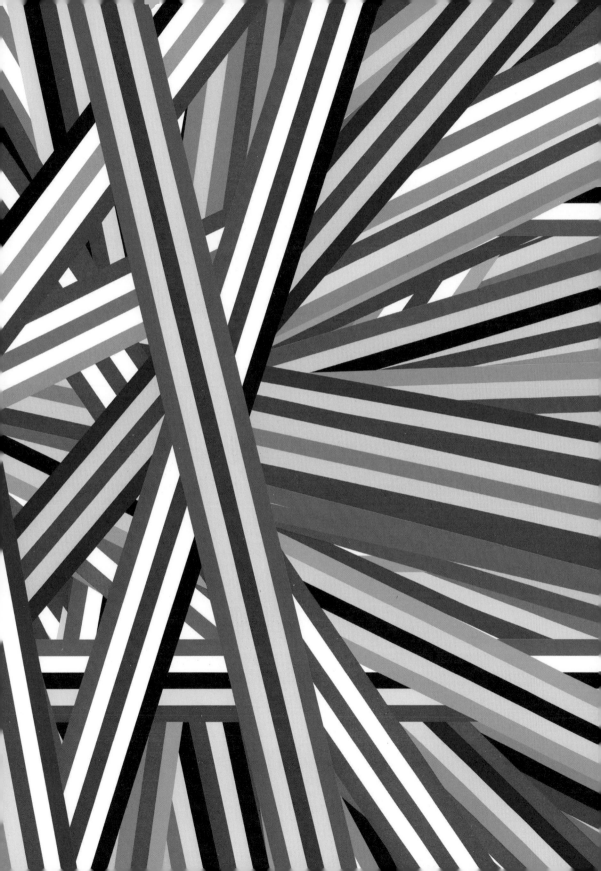

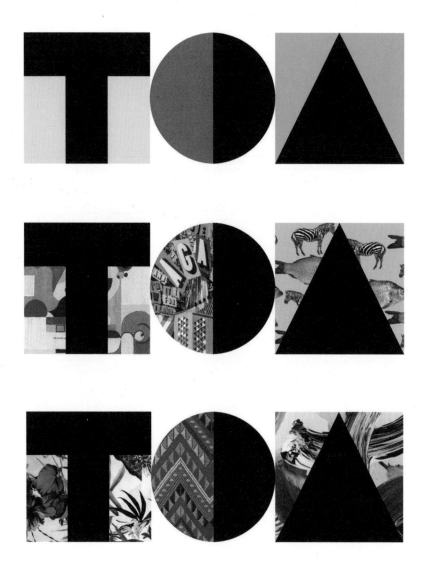

The Design Assemblage

Identity for an organisation providing
a programme of events & spaces for
the creative community
2020

ZA Rights – A Nelson Mandela Foundation 'Goodwill Collection'

Identity for a merchandise collection advocating for social justice
on behalf of a non-profit organisation
2020

Grow Hope

Billboard design for an initiative
to unite South African artists and
brands to create city artworks with
messages of hope & togetherness
2021

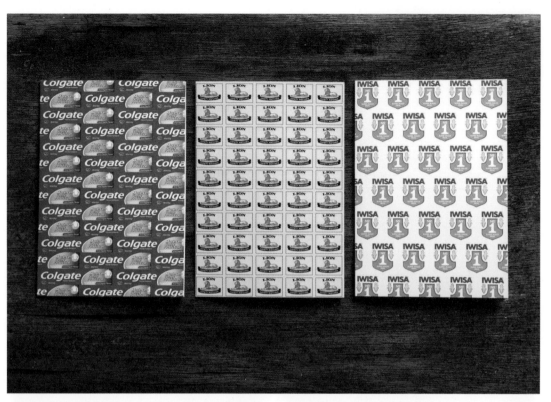

South African Greeting Cards

Locally-inspired South African
greeting card designs
2020

David Alabo

Incendies. 2021.

From Africa

davidalabo.com

Birth
2018

Instant Connection
2021

David Alabo

Peace
___
2021

Sunset Plays   Sculptor
───────────   ────────
2022   2018

MUTI

The World's Greatest Places for Time Magazine. Cover design for a magazine. 2019.

From Africa

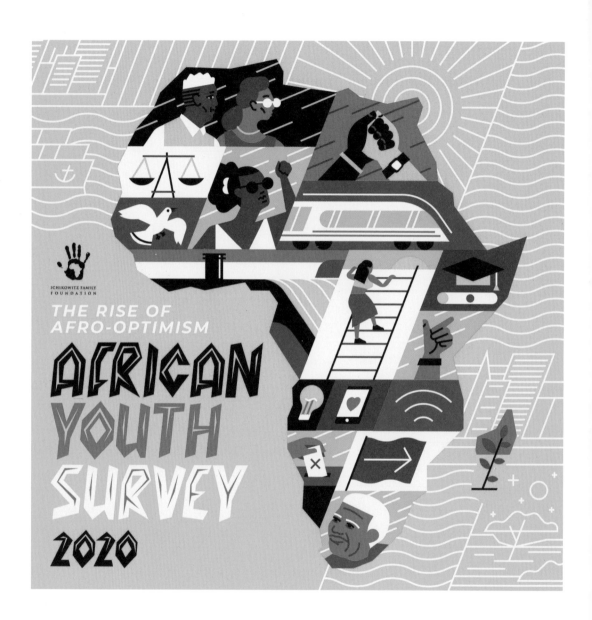

African Youth Survey

Illustrated guide for the 2020
African Youth Survey
2020

GoodGoodGood

Apparel
2017

→
The Hope Factory

Typographic artworks for
a non-profit organisation
2012

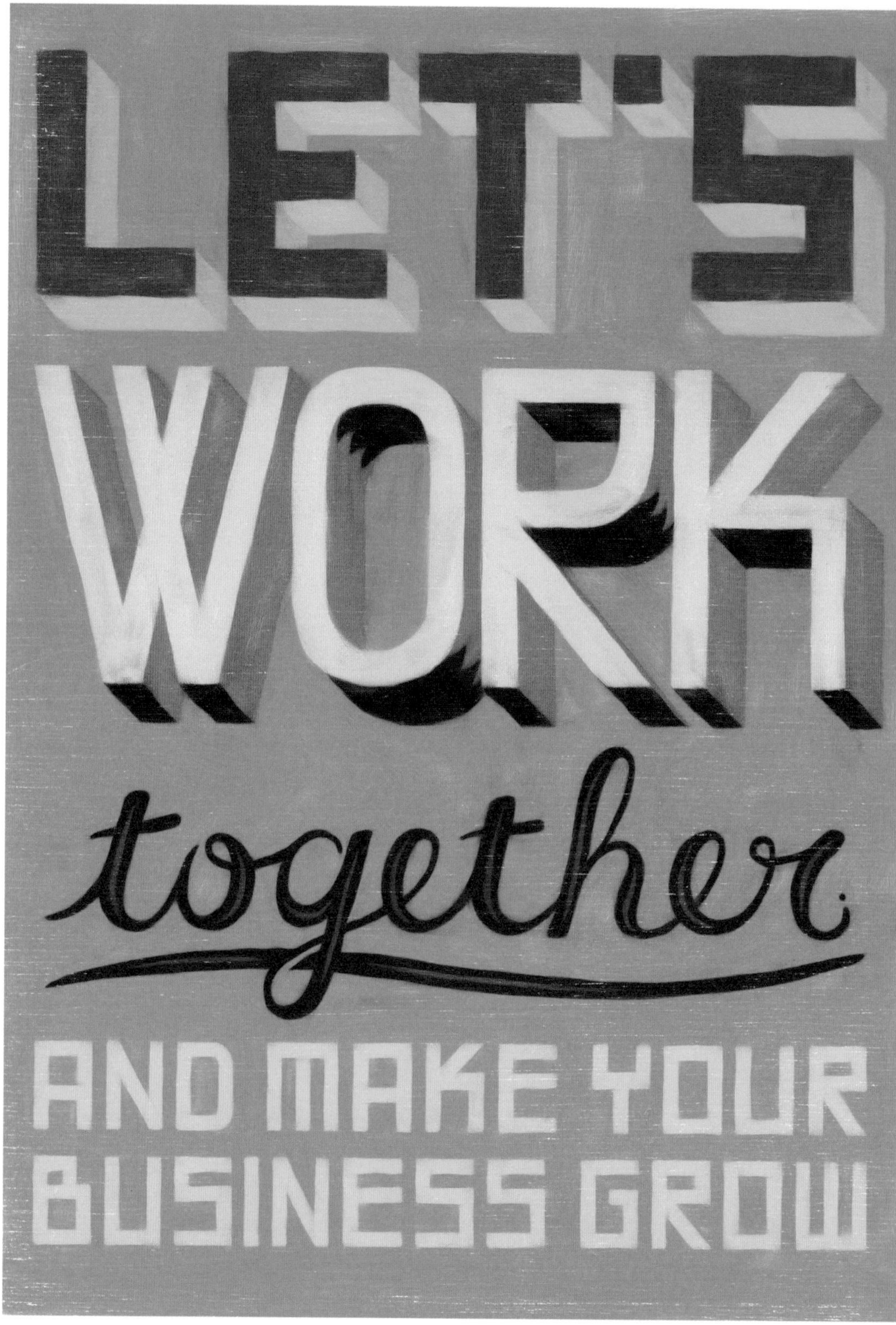
LET'S
WORK
together
AND MAKE YOUR
BUSINESS GROW

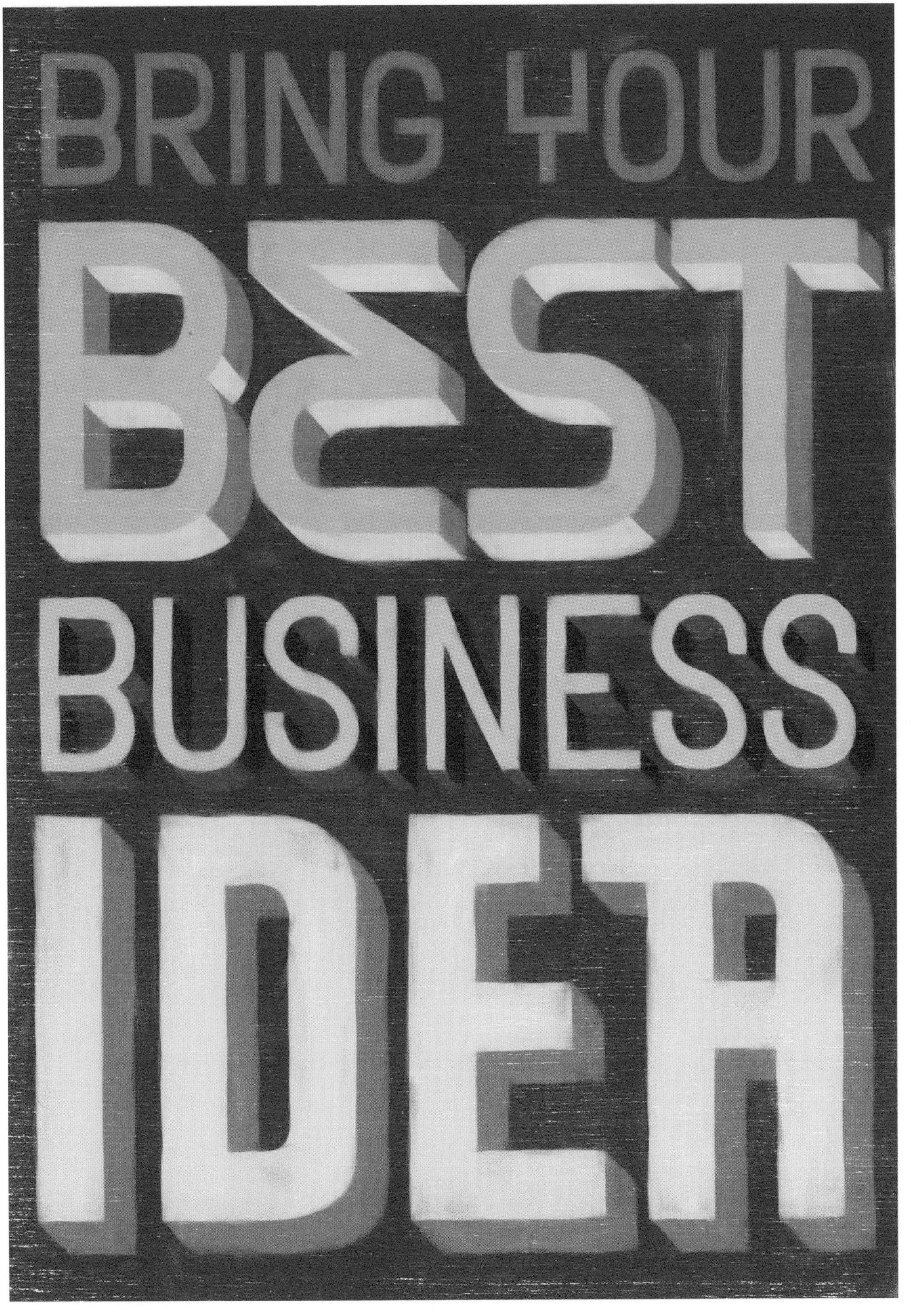
BRING YOUR
BEST
BUSINESS
IDEA

VUKA WAKE UP

EMAQANDENI

A NEW DAY is DAWNING

The DAY that can CHANGE YOUR LIFE

Vula! the DOORS ARE OPENING

FOR THOSE WHO HELP THEMSELVES

NOW IS THE TIME to PLANT, GROW & BEAR FRUIT

NOW IS THE TIME TO MAKE THE WORLD YOURS

the TIME to CHANGE YOUR LIFE

TO MAKE YOUR DREAMS COME TRUE

FOR YOUR CHILDREN AND THEIR CHILDREN

WHEN a DOOR OPENS

THE CHOICE TO WALK THROUGH

BELONGS TO YOU

The Hope Factory

SAICA Enterprise Development

MUTI

←
The Hope Factory
Typographic artwork for
a non-profit organisation
2012

Time Out
Cover design for a magazine
2018

Hust Wilson hustwilson.com
Thandiwe Muriu thandiwemuriu.com
Elio Moavero eliomoavero.com
Thabiso Ntuli thabisontuli.com
Vukile Batyi vukile-batyi.studio
Pearly Yon pearlyyon.com
Mam'Gobozi
Design Factory mamgobozidesign.com
Daniel Ting Chong danieltingchong.com
The Ninevites theninevites.com
Mrs + Mr Luke mrsandmrluke.com
Blood, Sweat + Polony bloodsweatandpolony.com
R!OT – Sindiso Nyoni studioriot.com
Bold Branding bold-branding.com
Studio Onss Mhirsi behance.net/onssmhirsi
Ahmad Hammoud hammoud3000.com
VM DSGN behance.net/vums
David Alabo davidalabo.com
MUTI studiomuti.co.za